The Art Of Critical Thinking

CW01023882

How To Build The Sharpest Reasoning Possible For Yourself

By

Christopher Hayes

Table of Contents

Introduction

Critical thinking is a way to improve your quality of thinking through rational and unbiased evaluation of factual evidence. These skills are used every day and they are extremely important in many daily situations.

As a beginner in critical thinking, it can be hard to know where to start. Some of the questions you might have are when can I use critical thinking, how do I practice it and why would it be useful to me in the first place?

However, once you understand the basics of critical thinking, the building blocks of creating arguments and are aware of the things that serve to completely derail critical thinking, you can begin to apply it to everyday life.

Once you know how to utilize the processes of critical thinking in real-time, you will see immense benefits to your life and will find that your thought processes become more efficient and organized.

As a researcher who makes a conscious effort to use critical thinking strategies as often as possible and understands the immense benefits it has to the quality of life, I am here to help you learn ways to improve your own critical thinking skills.

Critical thinking makes your life easier. It helps you to make better, more informed decisions whether you are buying a car, a house, choosing which university to attend or something as simple as choosing a gym to become a member of. If you begin to practice critical thinking daily, it becomes easier and you can begin to apply it to any situation that you find yourself in.

This book will tell you everything you need to know about applying critical thinking skills to your daily life. Not only will you learn exactly why critical thinking is essential for you to learn, but you will also find skills and strategies that you can practice every day to soon become a master thinker.

You might be thinking that critical thinking is too complicated and you will not be able to remember all of those techniques and use it in your everyday life. However, if you take it seriously and make a commitment to implementing critical thinking into your life, you will start to see some changes.

Like everything, it takes practice but fortunately, there are ways to break it down into easy steps.

You must remember that critical thinking is more of a mindset than a set technique. Before you know it, you will find yourself wondering why you ever found it difficult in the first place, but you won't get there if you wait any longer. Every moment you hesitate is a moment that critical thinking could have been used to benefit you.

You want to make changes in your life. You want to think in a way that is clear and organized and you want to make the best decisions for yourself. Don't hesitate a moment longer and find out how you can become a critical thinker now.

Importance Of Being A Critical Thinker

Oftentimes when people think of critical thinking, they picture using it in a classroom setting or at work on a major project, but critical thinking is so much more than that. People use critical thinking skills every day and it is vital to everyday life.

Critical thinking leads us to unlock our intellectual independence. By doing so, it moves people away from rushed conclusions, mystification and reluctance to question received wisdom, tradition and authority. It also moves people towards intellectual discipline, a clear expression of ideas and acceptance of personal responsibility for your thinking.

Considered to be the ability to think clearly and rationally about what to do or what to believe, critical thinking also includes one's ability to engage and reflect on situations. Most importantly, critical thinkers can engage in independent thinking. With this, they can form opinions by themselves through their perceptions and research instead of relying on others to form their opinions for them.

When a person takes the time to build their critical thinking skills, there are a few things that they can do that non-critical thinkers, otherwise known as passive thinkers, can't do or can't do very easily. These include: [4]

- Understanding logical connections between ideas.
- The ability to identify, construct and evaluate arguments for themselves.
- Detect inconsistencies in reasoning.
- Solve problems using a systematic approach.
- Reflect on the justification of the beliefs and values that they possess.

Knowledge is essential to critical thinking. This includes specific and general knowledge. The more you know about a topic, the more you will be able to think critically about it. However, critical thinking is about more than just accumulating knowledge. It is more about what you can do with that knowledge. A person can know everything in existence but if they do not know how to apply what they have learned, and then it is actually useless.

While forming arguments is another essential aspect of critical thinking, this does not mean that critical thinkers become callous and like to fight or be critical of other people. It revolves around improving theories, playing a role in constructive tasks and overcoming fallacies and other flawed arguments. It is also useful for improving work processes, social institutions and creative ideas.

The true importance of critical thinking, however, comes down to a few reasons.

- **It Enhances Language and Communication Skills**: Critical thinking plays a key role in how people communicate with each other. A lot of times we may not realize it at the moment, but the next time you are having an in-depth conversation with someone or giving a presentation, pay attention to your thought processes, what about it would you consider critical thinking and how you can improve those thought processes for next time.

Critical thinking serves to vastly improve how people form and express their ideas. It allows your mind to take the time to analyze and craft your ideas before expressing them clearly and concisely. It helps you to form well-developed arguments that are valid, strong, concise and cogent as well as creating strong premises that lead to supported conclusions. These processes are essential to think through your ideas and effectively communicating with those around you.

Additionally, critical thinking improves comprehension abilities. If you are reading something new and quite difficult to process, critical thinking is what allows you to analyze the logical structure of the text and help you to better comprehend the knowledge.

- **It Promotes Creativity**: Critical thinking and creativity go hand in hand. Critical thinking involves thinking clearly and rationally, following the rules of logic and scientific reasoning. However, creativity involves coming up with new and useful ideas as well as alternative possibilities. The two of them work together in the way that creativity is necessary to solve problems; however, critical thinking is essential when it comes to evaluating and improving these ideas.

  Coming up with creative solutions involve not only having new ideas but the new ideas must be useful and relevant to the task at hand. Suppose you need a new marketing strategy for your job. Creativity will be the key in coming up with the new strategy, but critical thinking will evaluate how good the strategy is looking at how it will affect the company long term and taking into account how your audience might react to it. So, when coming up with something new and innovative, you will find that critical thinking is very useful for selecting the best ideas and modifying them when necessary.

- **It Is Important for Self-Reflection**: It is important to justify and reflect on values and decisions in any situation in life. This is critical for living a meaningful life and structuring your life the way you want it to be structured. You may choose to live by a certain religion, a set of core values or following after the teachings or philosophies of a prominent person you admire. No matter what it may be that you choose to structure your life after, critical thinking plays a key role in that.

It is necessary to evaluate what that structure is

from an objective standpoint. This is how you avoid passive thinking. Without evaluating your life and what you live by critically, you will find yourself following others blindly without really thinking about what that means. From a critical thinking standpoint, you take control of your own life by evaluating and reflecting on yourself to discover what you should be doing and how you can improve yourself. This process is ongoing and this is how people evolve positively throughout their lifetime.

- **It Is A Domain-General Thinking Skill**: This means that critical thinking can apply to any category of thought. Critical thinking does not limit itself to one subject. Education, research, finance. Technology, management, law or science; you can apply critical thinking skills no matter what subject you are in. Being able to think well and solve problems is an asset for any career that you choose to go into.

- **It Is Useful for Interacting with Society**: Critical thinking is useful for the benefit of society; it improves how we interact and how we impact the world around us. Some examples of this are science, democracy and the current knowledge economy. Science may be the main field that people picture when it comes to critical thinking because of its use of experimentation and theory confirmation. The functioning of a democracy depends on people utilizing critical thinking skills because it informs the judgments people make and the things they vote on.

A lot of the world today is driven by information and technology, both things that also require vast critical thinking skills. These things require flexible intellectual skills and the ability to analyze information and solve problems. These are things that are important in a fast-paced and quickly changing workplace.

Critical thinking also informs the interaction people have with those around them. Instead of judging others, drawing false conclusions and being closed-minded about people who are different from us, if everyone utilized critical thinking skills, they would broaden their perspective and be much more welcoming to other people's point of view.

From there, people can work closely together to solve the problems of the world. The more people gathered from various and diverse disciplines, assembling to solve our many problems, the better our society will be prepared for the future. [4]

Critical thinking has seemingly endless benefits in a variety of situations. It is essential for getting the most out of life. When you implement critical thinking, you will find improvements across many aspects of your life from communication to education to interacting with society.

Now that you know how important critical thinking is, there are a few basic ways that you can implement critical thinking into your life daily. [3]

- **Watch**: Observing the world around you is a key first step to critical thinking. Watch what is going on around you, the people you encounter and how global, local and personal situations play out around you. Watching is also critical to a few important elements to critical thinking. One of them is broadening your perspective. This is very important to critical thinking because it allows you to see other people's points of view and expand your perspective so that you can form a more objective opinion about the world.

  Another key element of critical thinking that you pick up by watching is learning. Expansive knowledge is essential to critical thinking because you have more of a base to work with when developing arguments, conclusions and opinions. Watching is just one way of acquiring the necessary knowledge on a variety of topics and expands your means of critical thinking.

- **Think**: This might seem like the obvious answer when it comes to critical thinking. However, there are a few elements that make this more than simply thinking. As critical thinking is a metacognitive skill, meaning that it is a higher-level cognitive skill that involves thinking about thinking, you must follow the correct rules of reasoning if you want to think at this advanced level.

- **Dig Deeper**: This is the main action that sets critical thinkers apart from the rest of the crowd. Most people would come to the first solution that comes to their mind and that would be the end of it, but the critical thinker takes it a step further. The critical thinker does not settle for any conclusion and instead digs deeper and deeper until they find the answer that is completely satisfying and leaves no room for more questions.

- **Discuss**: The critical thinking process does not stop at your conclusion. One of the characteristics of a good critical thinker is that they are open to other points of view. Once you have come to your conclusion, it could be beneficial to discuss it with others.

   Discussing your thought process and conclusion with others can apply to several situations whether you are finding a solution to a work problem, doing a final presentation for school or even deciding what to do about redesigning your backyard. By hearing an outside perspective, you can explore other points of view and inform your conclusion.

You might find that there were flaws in your conclusion or something that you had not thought to take into account. This does not mean that your critical thinking was bad. On the contrary, this serves to enhance your critical thinking by bringing in an outside perspective which can give you ideas that you can incorporate into your next problem.

There are seven thinking habits, measured by the California Critical Thinking Disposition Inventory, which you should try to incorporate into your everyday thought process. Consistent practice of these can immensely improve the way you think.

- **Truth-Seeking**: Try to understand the way things are and if something does not seem right to you, make it a point to find the truth.

- **Open-Mindedness**: Be receptive to new ideas and even if you do not agree, give them a fair hearing.

- **Analyzing**: Attempt to understand the reasons behind things.

- **Systematicity**: Be systematic in your thinking. This involves breaking down complex problems into simpler parts.

- **Confidence in Reasoning**: Be confident in your judgment. Don't always turn to other people for validation and evaluate your thinking.

- **Inquisitiveness**: Be curious. Always ask questions, especially if you are not satisfied with an answer.

- **Mastery of Judgment**: Don't jump to conclusions and take into account the experiences of others.

The critical thinker does not rely on gut feelings and would rather figure out the answer to a question on their own without being handed the answer. This is what makes this step in the critical thinking process so crucial. Following the process of critical thinking, you would have at this point created a question for yourself and gathered all of your information and applied it to conclude. To dig deeper, this will require more research and eliminating any chance of outlying problems. Here, you might ask yourself a few questions to guide you:

- What conclusions can I draw given what I know?
- What can I rule out?
- What does this evidence imply?
- What additional information do I need to resolve this question?
- What are the consequences of doing things that way?
- What are some alternatives I haven't yet explored?
- Are there any undesirable consequences that I can and should foresee?[3]

Do This Whenever You Start Critical Thinking

There are a few characteristics that are essential to being a critical thinker. These include broad knowledge, the ability to examine reasoning and the biases around it, the ability to remain calm and collected in the face of uncertainty, and being properly informed about a subject. One of the most important characteristics a critical thinker can have, however, is curiosity.

The cliché saying is that "curiosity killed the cat" but the case of critical thinking is exactly the opposite. You could say that curiosity actually frees the cat because by being curious and asking questions, you open your mind to new possibilities.

When you ask the right questions, that is how you succeed as a thinker because questions are what powers our thinking in the first place. When you are told something or you learn something and you ask questions about it, your thought process does not stop at just taking what you learned at face value. When you ask questions, you gain more knowledge and that knowledge allows you to build a better argument, form your own opinions and avoid being a passive thinker.

How often does your mind wander? One moment you could be focused on one thing and the next, find yourself completely out of left field with your focus on something entirely unrelated. Asking questions serves to bring clarity to your thinking and set forth a defined agenda for your thinking. Questioning leads us in one direction and determines the information you are seeking. [21]

You can consider critical thinking a journey and questions are the steps towards your destination.

Overall, the importance of asking questions when putting critical thinking skills into play can be summed up in a few significant benefits: [5]

- **It Allows You to Explore Topics and Argue Points of View**: When talking with another person, asking questions allows you to carry the conversation on by creating a meaningful conversation with that person. By asking questions, you learn more about the other person's perspective which can, in the end, serve to inform your perspective on the subject. You can pursue a topic that appeals to you, defend ideas that are meaningful to yourself and sharpen your thinking skills.

- **It Gives You A Platform To Debate With Others**: Similar to arguing other points of view, asking questions allows you to debate your ideas with others which are useful because it provides a stimulus for learning as well as a reason for you to learn more about other topics. Also, asking questions keeps the conversation going; otherwise it would be pretty one-sided.

- **It Provides You with Information on Comprehension and Learning**: As you are engaged in a conversation, or even afterward, evaluate yourself in that situation and the critical thinking skills that you utilized. The types of questions you asked and the way you make sense of the answers are great determinants of how well you have comprehended what you just heard. This can help inform you of how well your critical thinking skills are coming along and what you can improve on.

- **It Allows You to Find Out What You Think**: As you ask questions, you also discover your opinions and reactions to what you are being told. Is this something that you can agree with or are you still skeptical? The more questions you ask, the more you will inform your conclusion on the topic.

When you think of back and forth question and answer

dialogue, one of the most common scenarios you may picture is the classroom. Most of us have experienced being in a class where the teacher asks questions to create an ongoing dialogue between the students and the students, in turn, ask questions to strengthen their knowledge and learn more from their peers.

Outside of a school environment, you can take those questioning skills and apply them to your critical thinking to further examine various topics through the use of application, analysis, evaluation and synthesis as well as gathering and recalling information.

One of the models used in the classroom which you can easily apply to your individual thought process was one used by Socrates where, through the use of questioning, he encouraged his students to explore prior-held beliefs and in turn to build stronger and more scholarly views.

While scholars using the Socratic Method were not

necessarily searching for a right or wrong answer in their students, the main idea was to inspire the students to reflect on their thinking. Respecting an individual's experiences, understandings and knowledge, Socrates believed that through questioning; previously attained knowledge could be used to develop a thinking which is supported by rationales and logic. [5]

As a critical thinker, self-reflection is imperative to our success in the practice of critical thinking. Critical thinking involves questioning our interpretations in addition to the interpretations of others. Every now and then, take time to examine your own beliefs and why you possess them.

Whether you are questioning yourself or the intentions and arguments of others, the answers that you find might inevitably raise new questions and that is when you know you have reached a milestone in critical thinking.

As you continue to develop your critical thinking skills, don't stop questioning. Question everything until you have all the reasons and arguments in the right place. Questions are even more important to critical thinking as they serve as a tool to skip the rhetorical talk and being manipulated by the media. [19]

When you are first starting out with developing your critical thinking skills, you might not be used to constantly asking questions about everything that happens around you. Luckily, there are a few basic questions that you can ask about any situation to start out.

There are questions that can be used in numerous life situations, and can help you make a deductive argument and conclusion. These are commonly referred to as the 5 W's and H questions. Not only are they easy to remember, but they leave room for the opportunity to open the door to many other follow-up questions. [9]

Question Who

This answers the questions of which individuals are involved in the conversation. When asking who, some of the questions that might come to mind are:

- Who benefits from this?
- Who is this harmful to?
- Who makes decisions about this?
- Who is most directly affected?
- Who would be the best person to consult etc.?

Let's apply this to a real-life example. Suppose one of your most intense passions in life is assisting children and your vision is to start a nonprofit where you can give children in need educational and enrichment services. When formulating a plan like this, a great place to start is asking questions. Not only will this lay the foundation for what you are doing, it will also help you to start working out the kinks of what your priorities are within the project. The 5 W's and H questions are a great place to start.

Starting with whom, the obvious answer is young children, but that's when you want to start going a bit deeper. Use the sub-questions as a guiding point and soon begin to develop your own questions in the who category. You might explore the specific age group you are trying to target, where they live, where they go to school and their income level. You would also look at who besides children would be involved in this project. This begins the chain of critical thinking.

Question What

The what questions are going to deal with the various functionalities, data, inputs, outputs, deliverables and artifacts of the topic. Some of the questions you would ask include:

- What are the strengths and weaknesses of this topic?
- What is the other perspective?
- What would be a counter argument?
- What is the best- and worst-case scenario?

Now apply these to our true to life example. This is an important phase when coming up with any kind of plan or strategy because it's when you really start getting into the logistics of it.

When starting these nonprofit things like strengths and weaknesses and best- and worst-case scenario are important topics to consider because it might end up being the guiding factor in your plan. Best case scenario, you have a flourishing organization that helps hundreds of children. Worst case scenario, it completely falls apart within weeks of getting started. What strategies are you thinking of putting into place to avoid the worst-case scenario? What would the rest of the community think? What would be your overall mission statement?

Question Where

This explores the geographic location of your topic. While this can seem simple on the surface, there are some in-depth questions you can ask as it relates to this.

- Where are similar situations?
- Where in the world would this be a problem?
- Where can we get more information?
- Where will this take us?

Looking at the nonprofit example, the most basic place to start is where should the organization be located, but then it gets a little more complicated than that. You'll want to look at where most of the children you will be working with are located and plan accordingly for where you will pace your own business. You may also want to consider whether you would have multiple locations or if you want to have a mobile business.

However, the questions asking where can go beyond just geographic location though. You would want to consider where others who have done similar endeavors located their businesses, where you can get advice, where you employees or volunteers would come from and where you see your business in the future.

Question When

This all comes down to the timing of your topic but, like the where questions, this can be more in-depth than what it seems to be on the surface.

- When would this cause a problem?
- When is the best time to take action?
- When will we know we've succeeded?
- When can we expect this to change?

- When should we ask for help with this?

Here you will explore basic questions such as when will you officially open, when will you meet with the children and when will you host events or classes?

Like the where questions, a little bit of critical thinking comes into play when you start to explore these questions further. You might consider whether the best time to take action is during the school year where children are immersed in academics or during the summer when they don't have the extra burden of school. When can you expect there to be downtime in the amount of people that you have participating and when can you expect the most people? When do you have children graduate from your program and when do you follow up with them?

When you know you have succeeded is also an essential question to ask. That's when you know you are doing the right thing with your organization but it will also let you know when you should start striving for more as to not become complacent.

Question Why

This deals with the various drivers or constraints placed upon your situation. Why is a critical question to ask when you embark on any plan or project? Anyone can say that they want to do something, but for it to truly be successful; there must be a reason for it. Some questions you can ask when you start asking why are:

- Why is this relevant to us or them?
- Why is this a problem or a challenge?
- Why have we allowed this to happen?
- Why has it been this way for so long?

Whenever you start a new project, initiative or even a new conversation topic, having a reason for it is essentially for the longevity of whatever that may be.

Think of any organization, business or service you know of, and try to imagine the reason that they came up with it in the first place. Cars? A faster way to get around. Internet? A way to communicate worldwide. There is a reason behind everything.

So, taking our real-world example, why start a nonprofit to provide services for children? Maybe you have noticed disparities among income levels in your community. Or there is a lack of enrichment services within the schools to benefit the children. You also want to explore why things are like this in order to begin coming up with long-term solutions to remove the problems completely.

Question How

By asking these questions, this is how you really get your project rolling. These questions require you to think deeply about what you are trying to accomplish, but they will be a guiding force to how you begin to implement your plans. Some of the questions you can ask by asking how are:

- How does this disrupt things?
- How do we know the truth about this?
- How does this benefit us or others?
- How do we see this in the future?

Think of the how questions are our real-life example of the real jumping off point to how you will really get into the process of putting your organization into action. First answering how you want to make changes in your community and how you want to benefit others is a great first step to thinking about what direction you want your plans to go in.

Then ask how you are going to implement your nonprofit, but you will want to be as specific as possible. Instead of simply asking how you will implement the project, but narrow down your questions to how do you want to start off, how you want the organization to run and how you will get people interested. [9]

Being Successful In Business

Picture the owner of a successful business. They sit in their office pondering the company that they run and the millions of questions that run through their mind daily on running their company in the best way possible and creating the best results for their customers and employees.

One of the situations at the forefront of their mind right now was the empty spaces in the company that needs to be filled with new employees. A stack of resumes and interview notes sit on their desk in front of them as the question remains of who would be the best person to hire for the job.

The company started at the beginning of the year and has been very successful six months into it. The goal now is to start expanding by creating more products and getting the company name out to more people. As the business owner, the question on their mind daily is what is the best way to do this? What strategy should the company use? What is standing in the way and what are the strengths and weaknesses of the ideas that the employees have already discussed?

Another thing that comes with that expansion is when is the best time to do it? The business owner, of course, wants to see the company flourish and wants to launch new initiatives at the right moment. Also, the company has laid out long-term goals and milestones and while everyone works hard to the best of their ability, it can be a long road getting there. When will all of the hard work pay off and when will they reach their peak of success?

One of those goals is opening a second location. The business has been doing so well lately, that opening a second location is possible in the near future. But where would be the best spot to open it in? Where is the perfect place that can reach old and new customers?

Despite all of the successes coming upon the company's first year in business, there have been some setbacks. This does not worry the business owner too deeply because they understand that every company will deal with some growing pains and bumps along the way. However, they do wonder why these setbacks have happened. Trying to figure out why will ensure that they do not happen again.

The business owner wonders all the time the perfect way to get the company booming to be the national and international business that they envision it as. How can they achieve these goals? How can they disrupt the market and make a splash with their products? How can they get to the top of their success?

The 5 W's and H questions can apply to any number of situations and workspaces. In business, employers and employees must ask these questions constantly to keep the business running smoothly but also reaching new heights as often as possible.

Yet, the world is ever-evolving and the world of business is constantly shifting. In today's world of fast-paced work, technology that changes on the dime and people who are constantly in the mindset of immediate gratification, the 5 W's and H questions are even more critical to the business world.

The better you can master elaborating on those six questions and applying them to your everyday life in the most efficient way possible, you will find that it will have a positive influence on your work. It will help to clear your mind and allow you to run your business endeavors even smoother because you will reach a sense of clarity within your mind that is not constantly cluttered with disorganization.

Filtering out extraneous information and focusing on the critical factors of your work in fast-moving industries, is a critical skill coming under the umbrella necessary to be labeled a critical thinker in the business world.

Consider the industry of content creation. In the digital world of today, content creation is hugely important for business because it allows the business to connect with its audience. This can include social media posts that encourage interaction from your audience, blog posts, videos, newsletters and more. The idea is to create quality content consistently to bring your audience closer to your business community.

The 5 W's and H questions can be instrumental in guiding ideas and create a guideline for content for the business. Following the basics of the six questions and the extended questions that come with it, you might also consider asking "what if?" as well. Here, you would ask yourself what if everything worked as it should, what if it didn't work out and what if this topic didn't exist?

With this process of brainstorming, and this goes for any business situation where you are trying to generate ideas, the key is not worrying too much about your ideas being perfect at this stage. Focus on quantity, not quality, and once you have all of these ideas written down, then you can start to filter out which ones are viable options.

In the case of the content creator, they would follow the guidelines of the 5 W's and the H questions, answering each one and writing down as many answers as they can come up with.

So, for the who questions, they might determine that the content creators and the consumers would benefit from the project, it is not harmful to anyone and the people who make the final decisions would be the supervisors and managers. For the when questions, they would brainstorm that the best time to take action would be at the beginning of the writing process and use brainstorming techniques before doing any writing and they will know they have succeeded when the content reaches their audience and people engage with it. And so on with the other questions.

Finally, they can take that opportunity to narrow down their answers into viable options that they can put into action. The final answer to the who question in this case would be the company's audience; what is the creation of quality content for the audience to consume; when is brainstorming ideas before the writing process and putting out the content when finished; where would be the company's website or other selected media platform; why would be to engage with their audience; and how would be by writing and creating engaging content. [9]

There are a few other strategies business people can implement into their daily critical thinking processes besides the 5 W's and H questions. Skills such as analytical thinking, developing interpersonal relationships and finding a sense of purpose are key elements in the critical thinking process that are often overlooked but are essential towards maximizing your critical thinking skills.

- **Being "Successful" Means Finding a Sense of Purpose**: People can have more fulfilling careers if we can focus on the purpose. This is the key to finding motivation and happiness in life. Once you identify your 'why' it's much easier to excel at your 'how.' After all, everything that is implemented successfully has a purpose to it and answering that critical why question is especially important to answer that question. This process also includes finding out the specifics of what is important instead of assuming that everything is important. This is where the process of narrowing down questions and coming to definitive conclusions in critical thinking comes in.

- **Be Wary of Assumptions**: Basing critical decisions on preset assumptions can cause an individual to overlook the important differences a particular group of people brings to the table. A critical thinker's curiosity is one of their most important characteristics. Instead of making assumptions — question everything. If you are not asking these questions and seeking out more, there may be better, more efficient and better styles that you never thought of before would be missing because you have just accepted the norm instead of finding out more for yourself

- **Focus on Resilience**: Another key characteristic of a critical thinker is to remain resilient in the face of adversity. This is an overall important life skill to have because when you find yourself blocked by any kind of obstacle, you can push through it and keep achieving. With a sense of resiliency, you understand that what worked before will not always work the next time. You know that you have to have more options and a broader palette. However, being resilient does not just mean being tough, it means being flexible in light of unforeseen scenarios. You may have something planned out down to the minutest detail but when something goes wrong and changes the trajectory of your plan, you do not give up. You adapt and find a new way to achieve your goals.

- **Be Honest About Your Biases**: There are a few ways to counteract bias. One is getting experience. Experiencing different parts of the world, different points of view, and different types of people is essential for broadening your perspective. The other way is to look for disconfirming evidence — this means actively search for it. If something does not go according to plan, find new ways to succeed in your ventures. If someone has an opposing viewpoint to yours, listen to them and attempt to understand. You might find out something new that you never would have thought of implementing before. Finally, take a look at your business and social circles and find a way to vary them so that you can discover new points of view.

- **Develop a Mitigation Strategy**: Some problems are not as easy to solve as they look to be on the surface. You can find the easy solution and fix it, but in the long run, the real problem will only be solved if you find out the core of the issue and solve it from there. Identifying the core problem involves studying the situation and developing a mitigation strategy. In this situation, it is critical to revisit that "Why" category and to ask the question, "Why might this not work?" By starting with this question, it allows people to build mitigation strategies on the front-end and to figure out alternative plans in advance.

- **Broaden Your Experience Set**: If you ever find yourself stereotyping, or over-generalizing based on your own experience, it is because your dataset is too narrow. The best solution to this is to go out of your way to spend time with people who are radically different than you. It might be uncomfortable, or even scary, at first. However, getting a sense of what others think and experience serves as a way for you to gain new experiences that you can use to improve your interactions with others. You should view new experiences as new opportunities. Branch out, listen to alternative viewpoints and keep a fresh outlook.[7]

Critical Thinking In The Professional World

Business is not the only profession where critical thinking is necessary. Critical thinking is essential to any profession you can think of. Retail? You will have to use critical thinking skills to solve problems daily and try to meet the needs of your customers. Journalism? You use critical thinking to evaluate the newsworthiness of a story and determine whether a story that seems simple on the outside has a deeper impact that needs to be explored. Trades? These involve utilizing a unique set of skills to create or fix things and solve problems as they arise.

Everywhere you go and with anything you do, critical thinking is a skill that is extremely necessary in all aspects of the workforce. It allows employers and employees to look at a situation from all angles and weigh every solution possible before coming up with a direct answer.

There are a few specific ways that critical thinking is beneficial to any profession: [23]

- **Coming Up with New Ideas**: Collaboration is a key factor that helps any company to stay afloat. There are few professions where you will not have to work with others at some point to come up with new ideas to benefit the company. Critical thinking brings about new ideas because you go in with an open mind and do not judge or dismiss the ideas of your co-workers before hearing what they have to say. Your ideas join with others to enhance them, and vice versa, and the group looks beyond conventional solutions to efficiently address problems.

- **Fostering Teamwork**: When everyone gets involved in the critical thinking process, the workplace becomes more efficient and organized as everyone is thinking to their fullest extent. Especially if the workplace is diverse, everyone brings their own experiences to the table and someone might bring in something that others would not have thought of before just because they have not had that same experience. Critical thinking promotes workplace tolerance and gives everyone a chance to have an impact on the future of the company.

- **Creates Options**: Not only does critical thinking encourage people to work together and come up with new ideas, but it allows people to come up with multiple solutions to one problem. The situation may require more than one solution that an individual may not have thought of otherwise, or it may only require one solution but the company has several options that they can now use to solve the problem. It also allows for the chance to use resources that are already available instead of having to spend money on new things. Additionally, it gives customers options as well.

- **Uncovers Spinoffs**: While the group is able to come up with options for one solution, critical thinking allows for completely new ideas to come out of those solutions. You and your co-workers may be talking about one thing and suddenly someone comes up with how that option can be applied to a completely different aspect of the company. Once you start asking questions and coming up with ideas, you can address other unsolved topics. [23]

While critical thinking can be generally applied to all professions at different levels, there are some professions where critical thinking is imperative to the success of not only the worker and the company, but the choices made through critical thinking have a major impact on the people they are involved with. In these professions, if the thinking is not critical and not supported by truth arguments, the consequences of that can be fatal or very dangerous.

Lawyer

Critical thinking is immensely important in this profession as lawyers have to make decisions in their cases that will have a direct impact on the futures of their clients. This involves using careful judgment and judicious evaluation. Lawyers have to be able to question and analyze what they hear, what they see, what they read, what they feel and what they think. Lawyers understand not to take first impressions at face value and dive a little deeper with a more thoughtful analysis.

Lawyers can make distinctions that the typical person would not see, see ambiguity while others see things very clearly, they can look at issues from all sides without actually stating their position, they can manipulate facts to persuasively argue any point and are often times better at analysis than decision making.

A lawyer must be good at deductive reasoning. This

means reasoning from general ideas to specific ones. In the case of a lawyer, this requires identifying issues, stating the general legal rules that apply to the issue and then analyze the facts in light of the rules of law to formulate conclusions to the case. [18]

Lawyers also use reasoning by analogy, which is a process is based on the idea that similar facts or principles should lead to similar conclusions. So, they will often look for analogies in other cases or fields of law to make arguments that are beneficial to their own clients. An example which illustrates this is an employer not being liable for the intentional torts of their employees. By analogy to a similar case, an employer should not be liable for the criminal conduct of their employees.

Another thing that lawyers do that is just as important as making analogies, is looking for distinctions in the facts or law and argue that adverse cases do not apply to their client's circumstances. [17]

Law is an expansive industry and there are a lot of different fields of law. However, no matter how different the field of law is, critical thinking skills are equally essential to each of them.

- **Civil Rights Law**: This field aims to find a balance between the government and individual liberties. While a small field, many lawyers who practice in other fields take up a secondary practice in civil rights law on a pro bono, or no-charge, basis. These kinds of lawyers often work for nonprofits, public interest law firms and law firms with diverse practices.

    One of the most famous civil rights cases was Brown vs. Board of Education which determined racial segregation in public schools in the United States was unconstitutional. Lawyers who supported Oliver Brown, the African American parent who led the charge for the lawsuit, would have had to use critical thinking to compile the key points of his case to persuasively argue their case against segregation in schools.

- **Corporate Law**: These fields of law focus on helping clients conduct their business affairs in a way that is consistent with the law, as well as efficient. Their responsibilities include preparing business initial articles of incorporation and handling a corporate reorganization under the provisions of federal bankruptcy law. The areas of corporate law include contracts, intellectual property, legislative compliance and liability matters.

  A famous example of corporate law was Dartmouth College vs. Woodward where the president of Dartmouth College was deposed by his employees and the legislature in New Hampshire then attempted to place the ability to appoint trustees to the school in the hands of the governor of the state. However, as the school was a private institution and the original charter of the school was created before the state was settled the nature of public versus private charters.

In the case of the lawyer who represented the case, critical thinking was necessary to use deductive reasoning to argue for the case of the school being a private entity and the timing of the creation of its charter.

- **Criminal Law**: This focuses on the fundamental issues of the law and personal liberties. Criminal lawyers defend the basic rights that are crucial to the preservation of a free and just society. The two main types of criminal lawyer are criminal defense lawyers who represent clients who are accused of a crime and prosecutors and district attorneys who represent the interests of the state in prosecuting those accused of a crime.

A high-profile criminal case in the United States, dubbed the Central Park Five, involved five teenage African American boys who were accused of raping a white woman in Central Park, New York. Although the boys were wrongfully found guilty and jailed for many years for the crime they did not commit, the lawyers representing them would have been responsible for proving their innocence. From a critical thinking standpoint, they would have used critical thinking to see the distinctions that would have pointed out the flaws in the argument that the boys were guilty and may have used analogies to other cases to prove them innocent. [8]

Doctor

Critical thinking is especially important as a doctor because the lives of their patients are in their hands - literally. The decisions doctors make are the difference between life and death for their patients.

They determine what medicine their patients need to keep their ailments at bay, the best types of treatment for various diseases and whether or not surgery is necessary to improve their condition. Therefore, critical thinking is essential to a doctor's effective decision making. [13]

Although there are so many innovations in modern medicine that include technology like robots and high-performance computing as well as things like molecular biology and DNA analysis, the power of critical thinking will always be important to the medical practice.

One of the most important steps towards treating a patient is properly diagnosing them with whatever medical failure they have so that the doctor knows how to proceed forward with the treatment process. Many medical errors are caused by cognitive missteps.

According to Jerome Groopman, a fellow of the American College of Physicians (ACP), and Endocrinologist Pamela Hartzband in an article for the medical publication ACP Internist, medical studies have shown that misdiagnosis occurs in around 15% to 20% of all cases, and that about 80% of these are characterized because of cognitive errors.

Critical thinking benefits medical practitioners in a number of ways. It helps them to avoid medical and clinical errors, identify better alternate options for diagnosis and treatment, it increases productivity, it leads to better clinical decision making, it helps them to work in resource limited settings, it leads to quality thinking and quality work output, it brings in innovation through creativity, helps to avoid litigations and serves to develop confidence in their practice.

Doctors must be skilled in the art of meta-cognition, or the ability to think about their thinking. This provides them with an understanding of how information can be misinterpreted or misleading, and awareness of this is more likely to reduce their own biases and cognitive pitfalls.

Making a correct diagnosis also involves arranging information from the patient's symptoms, signs and laboratory findings into a pattern, and applying it to a template of a typical case in the doctor's mind. With the assistance of medical textbooks and evidence-based protocols, clinicians use critical thinking to analyze the symptoms their patient is having and determine the likely diagnosis in typical cases. [10]

However, cases are not always easy to decipher, and may contain misleading information. In this case, critical thinking becomes even more important in attempting to determine the exact diagnosis, or returning to their analysis if indeed they are wrong. This resiliency is a critical thinking characteristic that is necessary for doctors to possess.

A perfect example of critical thinking in the medical field comes from the popular TV show House M.D. This show follows the main character, Dr. Gregory House, whose superb critical thinking skills help him to solve medical mysteries in his hospital. The vast majority of the time, his team is unable to come up with on their own because House possesses the ability to look at things from a unique angle and deeply analyze his cases to come up with the correct diagnosis.

Although Dr. House is quite cynical and has a lot of personal demons, there are a few key critical thinking skills that he uses in his diagnosis that are important for any doctor:

- **He Takes Risks**: Dr. House is constantly taking risks in his cases. Often times, everyone on his team believes one thing is wrong with their patient but House insists that it is something else. He follows that gut instinct to follow up on his premonition. If he didn't look beyond the surface of the patient's symptoms and go out on a limb against what everyone else says, many times he would not be able to diagnose his patients with the correct illness.

- **He Doesn't Always Follow the Rules**: One of the most defining characteristics of Greg House is that he does not follow the rules. Sometimes that gets him into major trouble. But sometimes, it epitomizes a special trait that any doctor could enact in their real life. Rules should always be broken with caution, but if it is necessary to come to a conclusion, a critical thinker will follow their instinct on it.

- **He Understands the Importance of Accuracy**: Accuracy is critical in the medical field; a misstep can be the deciding factor in a patient's life. Dr. House would go to great pains to ensure that his diagnosis and administration of treatment to a patient was accurate and when he was wrong, he immediately went back to the drawing board. He never settled for the obvious answer, such as the other doctors who would insist that numerous ailments were a result of lupus - until the one time it actually did turn out to be lupus.

- **He Knows the Dangers of Over-Analyzing**: We know that analyzing data is an important step in the critical thinking process. Over-analyzing, however, is when things can start to get out of hand. Your mind becomes fatigued, uneasiness starts to settle in and the critical thinking train starts to fall off the rail. While Dr. House spends a lot of time thinking about his cases, he also knows when to take a leisure break and come back to his cases, skills that can be useful to anyone. [15]

Judge

Think of how important the job of a judge is. Sitting on

the bench looking down at the defendant who could be in the courtroom for an endless set of reasons from reckless driving, drug charges or even murder, the judge is in charge of deciding their fate. The judge decides whether they go to jail and how long they stay there. The judge is the final determinant of whether the defendant is innocent or not. [1]

The judge decides a person's fate and because of that, critical thinking is essential in making those crucial decisions. They must look at the evidence laid out in front of them and evaluate it, analyze it, ask questions, consult with others and ultimately come to a final conclusion based on what they read and hear. They are in charge of finding the truth based on the evidence. If they did not use critical thinking in these decisions, if they did not go through all of the steps and look at the evidence from all angles using the best of their judgment, the consequences of their decision could be detrimental.

A few skills that the judge will use that require good critical thinking skills are:

- **Analytical Skills in Multidisciplinary Teams**: Not only will the judge need to analyze the case individually, there are a number of other people that come into play who the judge must take into consideration when they make their decision. They will need to synthesize information from the prosecutors, the jury and the testimony of the defendant and the plaintiff.

- **Research and Analysis**: Individually, the judge will need to analyze the information from all of those sources. They might even do a little of their own research looking back on previous cases for comparison or referring to certain established laws as guidance when they make their decision.

- **Looking at Problems from A Different Angle**: A judge requires critical thinking skills that use analytics and reasoning and part of that includes looking at a case in a different way than what may seem conventional. Maybe looking at it one way is not making any sense and looking at it from another would bring more clarity to the case. This also includes looking at different moral and ethical issues and figuring out the right questions to that that will lead the judge to the best solution. [14]

In court proceedings, the judge is not the only person who must use good critical thinking skills the jury must also use deep critical thinking skills. The jury is formed of people with different ways of thinking and judge has to rely on whether they have critical thinking and can make an impartial decision that has a massive impact on someone's life.

Throughout the jury process, the members of the jury will need to use their own critical thinking skills to come up with the best solution for the case. As part of the jury process they will:

- **Choose A Foreperson**: The foreperson serves as the spokesperson for the jury who will preside over the deliberations and present the jury's answer to the court. Choosing a foreperson requires critical thinking on the part of the whole jury as they determine who may have the most experience in law and criminal justice, or who has the best leadership skills.

- **Use Discretion with What They Can Bring into The Jury Room**: There are often strict rules about what the jury can and cannot bring into the deliberation room. These can include outside reading materials and cell phones. They can receive items for evidence such as medical reports, police reports and audio recordings, but certain personal items might be limited. Especially if the rules seem vague, it requires a person to size up the situation for themselves and make the best determination of what they should bring.

- **Determine When to Ask the Judge for Help**: The jury is allowed to ask for some assistance with their deliberation such as asking for a testimony to be re-read, asking questions about the law or about instructions on a point not already covered by the judge's instructions. This requires special judgment on the part of the members of the jury. They analyze the situation as best they can and if there are outstanding questions that none of them can answer; they determine that the best solution is to ask for help.

- **Deal with A Deadlock**: Coming to a deadlock is not ideal, of course, but it can happen. Every now and then, the best jury might not be able to reach a verdict. The judge can then declare a mistrial or order the jury to go back and try again. Critical thinking comes into play leading up to and determining the deadlock. Jurors go through the process of asking questions, examining evidence and debating amongst themselves. The critical thinking process is supposed to lead to a conclusion and if the conclusion is determined to be a deadlock, then that is what it is. However, it might also be the case where there are still outstanding questions that the jury has not explored so it would be useful to run through the critical thinking process again to be sure.[22]

Accountant

Critical thinking has been widely accepted as essential to most professions and accounting is no exception. Accountants work with a lot of spreadsheets and financial statements so critical thinking is useful in helping the accountant to interpret not only the numbers they see, but the story behind them.

Additionally, they need to be able to spot trends and irregularities in the documents they examine. Not only that, but they need to be able to come up with strategies to find solutions to those problems. Critical thinking would help an accountant think differently about finding solutions to the problems they see and come up with working strategies. [28]

Critical thinking is also useful in helping an accountant communicate with their clients effectively. For one thing, they need to be able to work effectively in teams, but they also need to be able to communicate well with their clients too, especially if they are not in the same physical location as often times they will communicate remotely.

They have to be able to explain the information clearly to their clients verbally and in writing. People come to accountants because they do not understand how to interpret the numbers themselves so the accountant must be able to explain it in a way that is easy to understand. [24]

These things combined help the accountant to become trustworthy to their clients as well as their co-workers. Accountants deal with sensitive information and careless mistakes can be detrimental, especially when working with a large company as their client.

To be an accountant requires specific skills and critical thinking can benefit all of them. Apart from specialized knowledge of accounting, simply general business knowledge is also important. This is a fundamental aspect of critical thinking because the more you know about a subject, then the better you can make decisions and evaluate information within that topic. With general knowledge, you have enough background information to refer to when someone tells you something that you would otherwise have to do more research on. With broad spectrum of knowledge, critical thinking becomes easier.

Critical thinking is useful in having the leadership skills required of an accountant as well. Critical thinkers have the ability to be leaders because they can think through problems clearly and efficiently, they do not get overwhelmed easily because they are able to organize their thought processes, they communicate efficiently and they possess critical thinking skills such as analyzing content, strategizing and explaining. Leadership skills are important in the accounting field because they must be able to develop new insights, manage projects, and motivate and engage team members.

As an accountant, critical thinking is also imperative in their customer service actions as well. Accountants work directly with clients to assist with their needs and this is where things such as communication become very important. In a public accounting firm, it helps to retain customers and bring in new clients. Critical thinking helps to determine when the accountant must listen to the needs of their customers, assess them and come up with solutions. [12]

Teacher

Although critical thinking is one of the most important

and necessary things for a teacher to teach their students, it is also important for the teacher to be well-equipped with critical thinking skills for themselves.

What ends up happening a lot of time when we talk about teachers is that people tend to focus on how much the students need to learn critical thinking and overlook the fact of how important critical thinking is to the actual teacher. The bottom line is that teachers cannot push students to think more critically if they do not do so themselves.

Think of it this way. Teachers encourage students to push their minds to think differently, seeking cooperative behavior from them in order to free them and allow them to express their ideas and opinions in a constructive manner.

However, oftentimes the teacher is expected to follow directions without their own autonomy and reasoning that comes from their own critical thinking. They spend a lot of extra time outside of the classroom studying teaching techniques and preparing lesson plans, but if they do not free their own minds, they are less likely to teach effectively. [27]

The creative instruction and innovation that really makes a teacher great comes from the teacher's own unique set of critical thinking skills that must be appreciated by not only the teacher, but the administrators and school system around them. To fully utilize the art form of teaching, the teacher must be fully engaged in the steps in critical thinking that allow them to do so.

Take for example a teacher who is developing a new course having to do with memoirs. No one in the school has ever taught a course like this before but the teacher has a strong passion for memoir and feels as though their students would benefit greatly from such a class.

The teacher must then develop the course from scratch. They must determine what they will read during the class, deciding what authors and memoirs would have the most benefit in moving the class along and teach different aspects of memoir as well as things the class can realistically read and discuss within the timeframe of the class.

They have to decide what work the class will do to reinforce the lessons they learn such as writing essays about the reading and work shopping their own memoirs over the course of the class and turning in a final memoir by the end of the class.

The teacher has to create rubrics, assessments and come up with questions they want the students to consider such as "Does the reading public's fascination with memoir suggest a healthy interest in other people" or "Does it too often indicate a voyeuristic urge to look through the debris of broken lives?" They might also take feedback and advice from their colleagues.

Finally, they must determine the end goal of what exactly they want their students to take away by the end of the class.

This seems like a lot of work, but it is all necessary work. The long and involved process of coming up with a curriculum for a brand-new class involves essential steps of critical thinking: asking a question, gathering information, evaluating the information, coming up with a solution, considering the implications and getting feedback from others.

Education in the United States lays out a set of common core standards that all teachers must abide by to ensure that students across the country are learning the same thing at the same time as much as is possible. The standards having to do with English/language arts, for example, have to do with analyzing complex texts, weighing evidence, making clear and effective arguments and to working with others with very different views.

Although there is a standard set of objectives that teachers of all grade levels have to abide by, this does not mean that they cannot make their own spin on it to make their classroom more engaging.

Because of this, these standards can only be successful if the teachers think as critically as the students are expected to. The teacher can follow the common core starts as closely as possible, but if they do not put forth critical thinking to make their class want to think critically as well, such as the case with the memoir teacher, then the students cannot be as successful.

The best way for a teacher to teach critical thinking is if they are proficient critical thinkers themselves. Sometimes the teacher might not like the answer of the student, but they have to agree with the logic if it includes critical thinking, have to teach children to do critical thinking with different methods, must increase the number of critical thinkers and improve social state of mind. [25]

Follow These Steps To Make Your Life Easier

The benefits of critical thinking in the corporate world are numerous. Whether you are an employee or the business owner, the decisions you make to ensure the success of the company require a certain level of critical thinking no matter the industry you are in, and in certain professions critical thinking can be the difference between life and death for the people you are helping or making decisions for.

However, critical thinking can be wildly beneficial in your private life as well. Consistently practicing critical thinking opens your mind, makes your thought processes stronger, improves how you see yourself and the world and lead to great academic performance and career progression. It is intentional and it is a specific mindset that drives people to discover concrete information that they can utilize in a practical sense.

Some of the ways that critical thinking can benefit your

personal life are:

- **It Allows You Make Better Reasoned Decisions**: Critical thinking helps you to better analyze complex problems with much more ease than you would otherwise. It also helps you to avoid the pitfalls of cognitive biases and fallacies.

- **It Helps You Develop Your Problem-Solving Skills**: Once you begin to use the critical thinking process in your everyday life, it will come to you much easier than ever before.

- **It Helps You to Become A Persuasive Communicator**: Critical thinking will teach you how to build logical and persuasive arguments. This includes developing premises that make sense and lead to conclusions that are sound, valid, cogent and strong. It can be an argumentative essay for school, an email or a direct debate with someone else. Critical thinking gives you a logical approach to being persuasive.

- **It Leads to Better Team Management**: With strong critical thinking skills, you will be able to distinguish between emotion and logic which is immensely helpful in developing a level-headed mindset that is necessary for leading others. It helps you to identify and solve problems effectively as well as drive performance based on sound reasoning. You don't have to think of this completely within a work perspective, sometimes you can find yourself in a leadership position among your family and friends that requires critical thinking.

- **It Makes You Immune to Bad Rhetoric**: No doubt you will encounter fallacies such as false dichotomy, poor arguments and people who utilize actions that serve to stop the productivity of critical thinking such as the intellectually arrogant or people who don't respect reason in the first place. Good critical thinkers can spot fallacies and cognitive biases and know how to not be blindsided by them. [16]

With numerous benefits to your personal life, critical thinking can be appealing but if you are a novice at the art, it can be hard to know where to start. The best thing to do is to utilize the critical thinking process as often as you can. Whenever you have to make a decision, follow the steps in the process and see how easy it comes to you over time.

The critical thinking process is essential for solving problems. The process that goes along with it is most often used with ill-defined problems; those that are complex and do not have an obvious answer or an expected solution. Although there is no correct answer to the problems, using the process of critical thinking you can come to a solution that is reasonable and valid.

These types of problems are the kind that requires a systematic approach, one that critical thinking is perfect for. Without this systematic approach, it would be more difficult or even impossible to reach a satisfactory conclusion that makes sense. So, to achieve the best results for whatever solution you are trying to find, you must follow the steps in the critical thinking process in order and carry them out thoroughly as all of the steps are necessary to reach a sound conclusion.

- **Formulate Your Question**: The first step in the critical thinking process is to formulate your question. This will help you to clarify the problem at hand.

    Knowing what you are looking for in solving a problem through critical thinking is an essential first step. A detailed question will guide you as you move forward in the process.

    To take a situation as an example, imagine that you have decided you want to live a healthier lifestyle and as part of that you want to join a gym. There are two gyms close to you that you want to choose from and both come with their own pros and cons.

So, the question that is posed to you is which gym you should choose?

One of the most important parts of this step is knowing what you are looking for and explaining it in detail in order to formulate a detailed question. Layout a list of criteria for you to make your decision. In this case of choosing between two different gyms to join, some of the things you might be looking for are the distance from home, how big it is, the amenities that they offer and how friendly the people there are.

- **Gather Your Information**: The next step in solving a problem through critical thinking is to gather all of your information. Information gathering helps you to weigh out the different options presented to you, moving closer to a decision that hits your goal.

Gather as many details as you can about the situation. These include the pros and cons, practical information and any questions you have about the situation. Explore any judgments, arguments, opinions and conclusions that you can find about the issue, whether this is looking online, reading it in a book or speaking directly with others. Ask yourself what evidence can you find about this that back up, or even disprove, your experience, beliefs or opinions on the topic.

Think of this phase as going through analysis and interpretation of the information you have gathered as well.

Also, at this step, you should be able to clarify the

problem or situation and ensure that you have a clear understanding of the issue you are trying to find a critical solution for. Ask the five W's and H questions to refine your thoughts on the issue. Some of these might include what is happening, who is involved, what are the stakes in the process and what is the best way to characterize, categorize or classify this?

To be even more thorough, into a deeper analysis of the matter at hand. Start to consider other perspectives, beliefs, assumptions and opinions apart from your own. Do this with an open mind so that you can consider as many options as possible. You should also analyze all of the facts and any metrics available to corroborate the evidence.

Some of the questions you can ask yourself are what are you claiming, why do you think that, what are the arguments (pros and cons), what assumptions must we make to accept that conclusion, what is your basis for saying that, what are the underlying or hidden issues and what would success look like for all of the people involved in the problem?

Be as thorough as possible about gathering information because it will inform your answers in the next step.

- **Apply the Information**: This is the stage when all of the information you found on the topic starts to come together. Asking a question and gathering information are considered the "Presentation of the Problem" aspect of solving a problem through critical thinking. When applying the information, this can be considered the "Taking Action" phase of the process.

  This is where you consider your reasoning and formulate a conclusion to the situation.

Additionally, you will try to evaluate the validity of your argument and solution.

During this phase you will identify and secure the elements needed to draw a reasonable conclusion. Here, you will compile all of the data, statements, principles, evidence, beliefs and opinions from the previous phases and begin to brainstorm ideas. At this point, you will identify possible conclusions and determine the viability of the conclusion you come up with.

At this phase, there are going to be critical questions you will want to ask yourself before coming to a definite conclusion on the issue.

Some of these are what conclusions can we draw given what I know, what can I rule out, what does this evidence imply, what additional information do I need to resolve this question, what are the consequences of doing things that way, what are some alternatives I haven't yet explored and are there any undesirable consequences that I can and should foresee?

- **Consider the Implications**: In this step you have come up with a solution to the problem at hand, but it is not enough to just settle on the first conclusion you come up with. Critical thinking in problem-solving goes way beyond that.

  Now it is time to consider the long-term effects of your decision. Perhaps right now it seems right, but what consequences will it have in years to come? This is the type of thing you want to think about before you settle with your decision permanently.

  This is all about assessing the credibility of the solution you came up within the "Apply the Information" phase. Here, you want to review any new evidence and ideas generated since you came up with your solution. Evaluate with fresh eyes the validity of the possible solution and probe for weaknesses in your thinking and logic.

Some of the questions you can ask yourself are how credible is the claim, how strong is the arguments, do we have your facts right, how confident can we be in your conclusion given what you now know, what are the consequences of this solution, what would it look like in a year if you implemented this solution?

A strategy you can take to guide the process of considering the implications is to start by recapping the critical thinking process, possible solutions and how you arrived at them. Think of any flaws that could have been present in your reasoning. Was there any bias in making the decision? Did you pass over or leave or any important information?

Finally, use the above questions to evaluate the validity of your argument or solution. If you can answer positively to most or all of the questions, then it is safe to say that the implications will not have any significant negative effects on you.

If you cannot answer positively to most of the questions, then it is time to backtrack and reevaluate your critical thinking process. This could mean that you need to gather more information or correct information. It could also mean that your question was not refined enough so you should go back to the beginning of the process.

- **Explore Other Points of View**: After you have considered the implications of your conclusion, the critical work is still not finished as you want to be completely sure that you are making the right choice.

This final phase is a chance for you to take a step out of the situation and look at it as a neutral person. Think of this as a moment to explore other alternatives to what you have come up with and see if you can come up with something better.

Exploring other points of view involves speaking to or reading about others who have a different point of view than you. One of the core aspects of critical thinking is being open-minded and able to explore other perspectives. This is very important for figuring out whether the decision you made is the best one and if there is a better one out there that someone else has come to that might fit you better. You might also determine that you can combine someone else's conclusion with yours to make an even stronger one.

Before coming to your final decision, really take the time to narrow down your decision and ensure that this is truly the best decision that you can come to before settling on your solution completely. Take the time to question, confirm, validate and connect your reasoning to your results.

Ask yourself if you can be more precise on your choice, how good was your methodology and how well did you follow it, how good is your evidence and is there anything that you are we missing before you commit to the decision.

Following this process of critical thinking carefully, you will be better equipped to make well-thought-out decisions on complex and ill-defined problems. Although sometimes it can seem like some problems that we face, critical thinking is unnecessary, it is something we use every day in either complex choices or issues that do not seem as complex such as selecting a gym to join. [29]

Everyday Life Eased By Critical Thinking

Critical thinking immense benefits to those who utilize it on a daily basis. It strengthens the mind allowing your thought processes to be more organized and bring clarity to your decisions. By practicing the steps in critical thinking as often as possible, in the long-term, you will find that you have an easier time solving problems, making reasoned decisions and you will have a much easier time communicating with others.

Although critical thinking has benefits to enhancing your mind, in a practical sense, it also has benefits in important life decisions that nearly everyone will find themselves making at some point.

Certain decisions that you make will have a huge long-term impact on your life and will have and the decision you make can either yield positive or negative effects on your going forward. Whether you are buying a house or choosing a place to go to school, you will find that critical thinking comes into play in making such important decisions. You must thoroughly analyze all of the evidence and consider the implications of all of the possible outcomes of what you are trying to do.

Buying A House

Critical thinking is especially necessary when buying a house because it is a long-term decision that will have an impact on you for possible years to come. Buying a house is one of the biggest investments that you can make so you must find a place that you can enjoy and be happy in for years to come. Otherwise, if you end up making the wrong decision and end up in a place that you do not like, you will either find yourself miserable living in that house or you will have to expend even more energy to sell the house and buy a new one immediately afterwards.

The steps to buying a house can seem complicated at first. There are a lot of things that you need to consider. Critical thinking will be important as you consider the quality and size of the house, the number of rooms, the size of kitchen depending of number of members in the family and more.

As you apply the steps of critical thinking to this decision there are some questions that you will want to consider as you get started. One of the most important is the location of the house. Do you want to live in a rural, suburban or urban area? Is there a particular city you are interested in? How far away do you want to live from your friends and family and from your job? If you have children, you also want to factor in school. What school system do you want to be a part of and how far from the school should you live? Do the children attend dance, music or any other extra-curricular activities? Also ask yourself what shops are close by and what the traffic is like in the area as well as what features you would like to see in the home.

Now gather and apply the information. One of those

factors will be finances. Determine how much the house will cost and how much you are willing to spend per month on mortgage. Gather your down payment and determine your credit score. A lot of research will be involved in the process as you search for the house at the price you want as well as a realtor.

Once you have gathered all of the necessary information, you've started working with your realtor and you have narrowed down a few homes that you might want to settle on, consider the implications. This is an important step in the critical thinking process, especially in a decision as big as this one. Is this a good place for you and your family to settle down in long-term based on the requirements that you have laid out for yourself? Weigh any pros and cons of the house and determine if there are any deal breakers within the cons. Have you gathered any new information and down it changes any of the information you have already collected?

Also consider looking at other points of view. What do other people think of the neighborhood and the city you are considering living in? If enough people have bad reviews, is it really something you want to take a risk on? Also get the opinions of family members. This might be especially important if you are a first-time homebuyer. If you have other family members who have more experience in buying a home, ask them for their advice before you make a final decision.

Choosing A Car

Transportation is a big deal, in some places more than others. In some cities, such as New York City or London, people can get away with not having a car because the area is so densely developed and the public transportation system is very efficient. However, in some places a car is essential. The public transportation system may not be very efficient, or might not even be available at all. Many places are not very pedestrian-friendly with not sidewalks or safe ways to cross the street. Also, certain cities are so spread out that walking several miles to simply get to a store is just not practical.

If you are the type of person who will rely on your car to get you everywhere from work to the grocery store and will use the car daily, choosing a good car will be absolutely essential to your success. You will use critical thinking skills to find a car that you can afford one that you will not have to spend a lot of money getting fixed all the time or on gas as well as one that if comfortable and contains the amenities that you want. Making a bad decision in choosing a car can have very expensive, and possibly dangerous, outcomes for you in the long run.

Applying the steps in critical thinking, the main thing you will want to ask yourself in the beginning is, what do you want in a car? For most people, the price will be the first thing they look at. Determine if you want to pay for the car in full upfront or do you want to put in a down payment and take on a car note. You will also want to consider if you have any preferences to the type of car and the size. If it will just be you in the car most of the time you might want to go for a smaller car. If you have kids, you would consider a larger car. You would also consider where you want a car that is run on gasoline or diesel fuel. For example, diesel costs less, but diesel cars are being banned in the EU due to pollution, so it will not be possible to sell it in the future and so on.

Now begin to gather and apply all of your information. Like purchasing a house, a lot of research will go into this stage. You could go online to search for different types of cars or you can even go into the shop to take a look in person. Determine the car dealer you will want to go to and even if there is a particular salesperson you want to help you. Start getting your finances worked out, analyzing your credit score and having the car financed with your bank.

As you go through the process of picking out the car,

start considering the implications. Is the price of the car something you can follow up on as you continue to make payments on the car? How does the car feel when you test drive it? Do you foresee any mechanical issues with the car that you will have to spend money to fix later on down the road? These are all questions you want to ask as you consider the implications of the car.

Looking at other points of view is a good idea when choosing a car as well. Review can be very useful in this process. Look at reviews of not only the particular model of the car but the dealer where you will be purchasing the car as well. If a significant amount of reviews has had a problem with either, it might be a good idea to reconsider. Also, if it is your first time buying a car or you do not have much experience with buying a car, ask a friend or family member who knows more about cars to help you. This can be helpful in ensuring that you are not overcharged or ripped off in some way, but use your own judgment as well in the process.

Choosing University

The university that you choose to go to has major implications on the new four years or so of your life. The type of education that you get there determines the trajectory of your career path. The kinds of professors and classes you take will have implications on the knowledge you gain on the subject and, in a lot of cases, whether you continue it in the first place. Not only does it mean a lot for your education, the university you go to also has a lot to do with your lifestyle. If you will be living on campus, it can have an impact on your personal and social life and if you decide to live off campus, your commute can have an impact on your lifestyle as well.

Critical thinking is huge when making such a big decision. If you do not use your critical thinking skills in making such a big decision, it can have a very negative impact on your personal life and education. You might find that this is not the best school for the major that you choose and because you are not learning in the way you think you should, you do not get the most out of the money you spend on those classes. Worst case scenario you might be deterred from pursuing the major further and end up quitting. Additionally, if you do not like the social environment of you school, you could end up feeling lonely and depressed.

In making the wrong decision choosing a university, if you decide to transfer to one that better suits you, you will not only have to spend the extra time going through the process of choosing a school again, you may end up having to spend more time in school than you originally intended. People spend way too much money on going to a university for it to not be a decision that they are comfortable with.

As you are choosing a university to attend, there are a lot of questions that you will want to explore as you move forward with the process. One of the major questions will be your major, whether the university offers it and in what capacity. Also ask yourself what are the most required professions currently and can one anticipate will the profession be still attractive in the future after one has graduated and does it comply with your talents and affections. Some other questions to consider are the cost and what kind of financial assistance is available, whether you would prefer a large or small school, whether you want to stay on campus or commute and what the on-campus housing is like if you prefer to stay on campus.

Gather all of the information you can about the school. This includes how much it costs to attend the school per year in addition to either how much it costs to live at the school or what the commute will be like (traffic conditions, campus parking, distance). Fill out your FAFSA and any other information needed to gain financial assistance. Determine the requirements for your major at that school and develop a preliminary plan of what you will need to do over the next four years. In addition, you should look at what the school environment is like and what extracurriculars appeal to you.

Critical thinking will also come in handy here when you determine the implications of going to the school. Looking at your own lifestyle and finances, you will determine how you will pay for the education and whether you need to make any changes in order to afford it. In some cases, it will take more than four years to graduate and consider if this is something you are willing to do or would you prefer a different option where you can actually finish in four years.

When it comes to choosing a university, hearing feedback from others is always a good idea. Some people have better experiences at the school than others but if you find that things like the food options, the housing arrangements or the kind of professors do not resonate with you as much as they have with someone else, you might rethink things.

Do This To Stop Questioning Yourself

Critical thinkers tend to revise their decision less than other people. They are certain of their decisions because they have analyzed arguments in detail.

For one thing, those that use critical thinking have much stronger reasoning skills. Reasoning determines how good people are at decision making because it involves clear problem solving and the formation of logically persuasive communication, skills that are equally important in all functional domains. Logical reasoning is a learned skill, it takes years of practice, depending on the person. It is a learned skill that is based on an already established body of knowledge.

Another reason that critical thinkers do not question themselves as much is because they are aware that their perceptions are biased so they take the time to reflect on them, analyze their flaws and merits and make decisions outside of perceptions that are not beneficial to the situation at hand.

People naturally have biases that they are not aware of or are not educated about. Because of this, decisions are based on an incorrect judgment about a situation or bad inferences that come from these biases.

Imagine a person who is trying to decide on a university to attend. They were accepted into one of the top schools in their state but are reluctant to go because their perception of the town it is located in has always been bad. A decision influenced by the people around them because this person has never actually been to this town, they are not aware that this is a nice place to live but because of their internal bias, they are constantly second-guessing whether they should go to this school and might end up deciding not to go entirely.

Now imagine the person who has strong critical thinking skills. They were also accepted into the top school in the state and has also developed a negative perception of this town because of the influence of those around them. However, because they are aware of their bias and have strong reasoning skills, they decide to do a little research of their own before they make their final decision. They consult reviews of the place, ask people who have more experience there and even go and visit themselves to get firsthand experience. From there, they can confidently decide to attend school without any regrets.

Finally, critical thinkers can separate logical reasoning from emotions and moral judgment. A lot of times, people are more easily swayed by emotions and morals than logical reasoning. These things appeal more to the senses as well as a person's feelings of guilt and they can give into these things more easily, even if the decision is the wrong one.

Take another real-life example for instance. Someone's brother is asking them for money. They were recently laid off from work and their savings are quickly running dry. However, the brother is a known alcoholic and as much as they try to deny it, the brother is going to spend the money to buy more alcohol.

This person then goes back and forth in their decision on whether to give their brother money. On one hand, if they give the brother money he will continue to drink, come to rely on them more for money in the future and possibly end up getting hurt or arrested because of the drinking.

However, the situation appeals to the emotions because if they don't give the brother money he may resort to other, more illegal means to get it, or might get depressed and hurt himself in another way. Do they continue to enable their brother to drink or do they stop supplying him with money in the hope that he will hit rock bottom and want to get help? Against their better judgment, they may continue to enable the brother to drink in the interest of making their brother feel better.

Critical thinking is a strong force against decisions influenced by emotions or moral judgment. Significant knowledge of rhetoric, rhetorical devices and a perspective on moral reasoning comes a long way in making rational and logical, especially when appeals to emotion or moral judgments are made.

Whether in a workplace situation or your personal life, critical thinking is essential for any form of decision making. Not only that but it helps you make much stronger decisions and be surer of yourself.

However, there are a few things that can very easily sabotage critical decision making. These include fallacies such as:

- **Hasty Generalization**: This is a conclusion that is not logically justified by sufficient or unbiased evidence.

- **Perfectionist Fallacy**: This fallacy assumes that a perfect solution exists and that you should keep searching for it before taking action.

- **Line Drawing Fallacy**: This presents the alternatives as either there is a precise line to be drawn, or else there is no line to be drawn, or there is no difference between one end of the line and the other.

- **Groupthink and Bandwagon Effects**: This is the act or practice of reasoning or decision-making by a group. It is especially characterized by uncritical acceptance or conformity to the most prominent points of view.

- **Ad Hominem Fallacy**: This is a way to divert attention from a genuine discussion of the topic at hand by instead attacking the character, motive or another attribute of the person making the argument.

- **Base Rate Neglect**: When presented with related base rate information and specific information, the mind will tend to ignore the former and focus on the latter.

Critical decision making can also be sabotaged by cognitive biases. Some of these include:

- **Confirmation Bias**: This is the tendency to interpret new evidence as confirmation of one's existing beliefs or theories.

- **Survivorship Bias**: This involves people concentrating on the people or things that made it past some selection process and overlooking those that did not, usually because of their lack of visibility.

- **Anchoring**: Here people depend too heavily on an initial piece of information offered when making decisions.

- **Availability Bias**: This is a tendency to think that examples of things that easily come to mind are more representative of real-life than is the case.

- **Authority Bias**: This is when people attribute greater accuracy to the opinion of an authority figure and be more influenced by that opinion.

- **Projection Bias**: People assume that their tastes or preferences will stay the same over time. [16]

People who use critical thinking can identify fallacies and cognitive biases and avoid them to make better and more confident decisions. After the decision is made, true critical thinkers rarely revise it because they think far ahead.

They are able to tell themselves things like "I am now logical and analytical with all the information that comes to me and has opened up all sorts of areas of growth for me," "I understand people better and have a much greater insight into the motivations of man," "I am much better at problem-solving and it impacts my life from grocery shopping to cutting through the crap in a Black Friday advertisement" and "I have increased confidence and authority on many subjects because I can see deeper into them than other people."

A Guaranteed Way To Improve Your Critical Thinking

There are points which are very important to keep up with if you wish to be critical thinker. They are:

1. **Grounding Your Thinking**: This is a technique that helps to keep your mind in the present instead of letting it wander around aimlessly to different topics. They are especially helpful in helping someone to reduce anxiety as well as mental focus from a highly emotional state. There are two different approaches you can take to grounding your thinking: sensory awareness and cognitive awareness. You can utilize sensory awareness by honing in on the five senses: noticing your surroundings, holding something with a significant texture, listening to soothing music, etc. For cognitive awareness, you can reorient yourself to your surroundings by asking yourself a series of questions such as where am I, what is today, what is the date, how old am and what season is it? [11]

2. **Understand Simple Things Deeply**: This is what critical thinking is all about. To get some practice, there is an easy way to practice it every day. Just take something simple like nature, children playing or people you see while you're out shopping, and try to analyze it a little bit deeper. An easy way to do this is to apply the 5 W's and H questions to it. For example, you notice a few deer roaming around your yard. It seems like a basic thing but ask those six questions to analyze it a little deeper. Who led them there? What are they looking for? When do they come out into the open every day? Where do they like to find food? Why did they come to your yard? How do they determine where they wander?

3. **Clear the Clutter – Seek the Essential**: An important aspect of critical thinking is being organized and seeking clarity in your thoughts. First practice this in practical situations such as keeping your house free of clutter or keeping your work desk organized. When you practice such

actions daily, it makes it easier to translate that to your mind. Mentally, practice keeping your mind free of any unnecessary information. For example, when grocery shopping, only focus on the groceries that you actually need to get, do not clutter your mind with thinking about buying extra things that you don't really need.

4. **See What's There**: Practice awareness in your everyday life by staying focused on your surroundings and making informed observations. Wherever you are, take a moment to notice your surroundings and see what is currently there. Are there any particular people you are interested in? What is the scenery like?

5. **See What's Missing**: While taking notice of what is a part of your surroundings, also take the time to notice what is not there. Observe if there is something or someone that should be there but is not or things that you were expecting to see.

6. **Final Thoughts: Deeper Thinking Is Better**: No matter what it is that you come across in your life, attempt to find a way to see it for more than what it is on the surface. A deeper analysis of a certain object or situation will give you an opportunity to practice critical thinking and when a real critical thinking situation comes into play you will be prepared.

7. **Igniting Insights Through Mistakes**: One of life's greatest lessons is making mistakes. So, when you make a mistake, don't give up, don't feel down on yourself or scold yourself for it. Instead, take the time to step back from it and examine it. Determine what the situation was and what exactly went wrong. Ask yourself how you could have done better in that situation and come up with some ideas about what you can do the next time you are in a similar situation to ensure that you do not make the same mistake again. Finally, determine what you have

learned from the mistake that you can take into much different situations.

8. **Welcome Accidental Missteps – Let Errors Be Your Guide**: Embrace the mistakes that come into your life. Accept that not everything is going to go perfectly and that accidents and missteps happen to everyone. No one is immune. Also understand that those things make you stronger. Apply the lessons that you learn from them to the next situation you encounter whether it is similar or not.

9. **Finding the Right Question to the Wrong Answer**: Suppose you are trying to find a solution and you come to one that does not exactly work. It's time to go back to the drawing board but what should you change about your process to lead to the right answer this time? A good first step is coming up with a different question. Finding the right question is important because once you find the

right question, the right answer will come more naturally to you. It brings clarity and focus to the issue while lighting up the path to the right solution.

10. **Failing by Intent**: Being intentional about your decisions means you are being active in your decision making. So, if there is something you are planning on doing but it ends up not working out, it is more beneficial to have been intentional in the actions leading up to it.

11. **Final Thoughts: A Modified Mind-Set**: There are times where you make a goal to do something, such as waking up early in the morning to exercise, but by the time the alarm goes off, the motivation to get up and exercise is gone and you do not want to do it anymore. Instead of simply saying you don't feel like it, make sure you have good specific reasons for modifying your mindset. In this case, you could say you were interrupted and did not get

as much sleep as you intended or your mood changed, but make sure you have good reasons for changing your mind.

12. **Creating Questions Out of Thin Air**: Sometimes it is necessary to ask questions but the exact question you want to ask does not come very easily to you. When trying to come up with a question out of thin air, you want to think from general to specific. Think of the key points of the situation. For example, your grades are low and you need to figure out a way to learn more effectively so you can get them up to at least a B in order to pass the class. Now that you know the general situation, determine the most important factors in that scenario. Here it would be, "How can I study more effectively in order to pass this class?"

13. **How Answers Can Lead to Questions**: Answers can be the stimulus for more questions to be asked. Have you ever been in a classroom

situation where a student asks one question and after the teacher answers, more hands shoot up one by one to ask more questions based off of that one answer and the conversation continues in that way? This is because when asking one question, the answer can lead to something you had never thought of before or something else that you want to know.

14. **Creating Questions Enlivens Your Curiosity**: Think of a small child that keeps asking questions. They want to know why the sky is blue and once you give them an answer they ask why and they continue to ask why until you run out of answers for them and have to change the subject. Children are naturally curious and have no insecurities when it comes to the amount of questions they ask. Adults can be just as curious. Especially when one question raises even more of them and you just have to know the answer until you are fully satisfied. When you desire to know something, imagine being the innocent child who wants to know why and come

up with more questions until you reach the satisfying answer.

15. **What's The Real Question?**: Although you can come up with questions out of thin air and ask more than one question, the end goal should be to get to the real question. This is the true focal point of your curiosity, the central point that will lead to your conclusion. Getting there might involve asking many questions until you get down to the right one, but the main initiative should be to answer the real question before you form a conclusion.

16. **Final Thoughts: The Art of Creating Questions and Active Listening**: Creating multiple questions is fine, but just as important is listening to the answers to those questions. This not only prevents you from asking unnecessary questions, but when you fully listen to the answers you gather more data to inform your next question and ultimately come to your conclusion.

17. **Seeing the Flow of Ideas**: The formation of ideas and acting on them is what ultimately leads to a sound conclusion. Oftentimes, the first idea is not going to be the solution that you settle on. Like questions, one idea will build off of another until you finally reach a satisfying idea that you have analyzed thoroughly and see a way that it can practically be carried out. Imagine a work situation where the group is coming up with ideas to grow the company. One employee gives their idea, and the next employee comes up with a way to make it better. A few more people might share their input until the group realizes that this might not be entirely viable in the end but the next idea uses certain pieces of the last one and the group builds on that instead. The end result is a mixture of all of the ideas that were suggested and discussed.

18. **Understanding Current Ideas Through the Flow of Ideas**: The flow of ideas also helps you to understand more about the current idea that is

being used. Suppose at this same business, one idea is already being put into practice to grow the company but the employer feels like it could be better. Through the flow of ideas, the group discusses what to do, they realize ways that the current idea is not working and how they can improve it.

19. **Creating New Ideas from Old Ones**: Although an old idea may not be carrying out goals in an idea way, they provide a basis for new ideas to be formed. The idea as a whole may not be working, but there could be certain aspects of it that are still very good and you can build off of those in order to form an entirely new idea.

20. **Final Thoughts: "Under Construction" Is the Norm**: Sometimes there is not just one final solution or the final solution takes a long time to get to. Different ideas are pitched and put into practice that build off the last idea and while they may show

some progress, they do not get you to where you want to go and you have to modify it.

21. **Engaging Change**: Change is imminent. It's not something you can fight; it comes no matter what. It is how you handle change that makes a difference in the outcome. The critical thinker embraces change. They are open-minded and do not let change deter them from making progress. In the process of change, they accept mistakes, ask questions and come up with new ideas in an attempt to make the best of it and come up with something better.

The Best Way To Get Started

Like anything, you cannot realistically expect to be amazing at critical thinking the first time you try it. If you are, then that's amazing, but for most people that won't be the case and there is nothing wrong with that. For the hew critical thinker, the best way to get better is to practice. The phrase "practice makes perfect" heavily applies to critical thinking.

Your development as a critical thinker will likely be a gradual process and you will find that you go through phases as you progress. Before getting started, consider yourself the unreflective thinker where you are unaware of the immense benefits of critical thinking. When you just start practicing you will become the challenged thinker where you have recognized the problems in your thinking and have taken on the challenge of becoming a critical thinker.

From there you will be a beginner in critical thinking where you have minimal critical thinking skills, then a practiced critical thinker where you are getting regular practice and then the advanced critical thinker where you have become advanced in your skills.

Once you become really good at critical thinking, the final stage in the development of critical thinking is the master thinker. At this point the skills and insight that come with critical thinking become second nature to you.

If you are reading this book, likely you are in the challenged thinker phase where you recognize the flaws in how you have been thinking and understand the benefits to your life that will come with improving your thinking.

As you begin your critical thinking journey, there are a few exercises you can put into practice every day so you can cultivate your skills and start moving towards being a master thinker.

Use "Wasted" Time: People often fail to use all of their time productively. Naturally, they want a moment to just take a break, let their minds wander aimlessly and decompress from a long day. While taking a break is often very necessary, sometimes wasted time becomes a negative thing. You jump from one diversion to another without actually enjoying it, you become upset about things you cannot control or you worry unproductively.

Instead of letting wasted time turn into a negative consequence, use it productively by taking the chance to practice critical thinking. So instead of wasting your time browsing through Netflix without actually finding anything worthwhile to watch or spending time aimlessly scrolling through social media, use it to do some self-reflection. Think over your day and some of your strengths and weaknesses.

There are a few questions you can ask yourself such as when did I do my worst thinking today, when did I do my best, what in fact did I think about today, did I figure anything out, did I allow any negative thinking to frustrate me unnecessarily, if I had to repeat today what would I do differently and why? Take it a step further by recording your answers. This way you can really dig deep and reflect.

A Problem A Day: Make it a goal to solve one problem each day. At the beginning of the day, choose a problem to work on when you have free moments throughout the day. Figure out the logic and identify its elements. Some of the questions you can ask yourself in that process are what is the problem and how can I put it into the form of a question and how does it relate to my goals, purposes and needs?

Follow this process when solving the problem:

- Take your problems one by one stating is as clearly and precisely as possible.
- Study the problem to make clear the "kind" of problem you are dealing with. This involves

figuring out the kind of things you will have to do to solve it and distinguishing them over something you can control versus something you cannot.

- Determine the information you need and actively seek it.

- Collect information and analyze and interpret it carefully. Draw any reasonable inferences.

- Figure out your options for taking action. Make plans for what can you do in the short term and long term and recognize your limitations as far as money, time and power go.

- Evaluate your options. Take into account the advantages and disadvantages of those options in the situation you are in.

- Develop a strategic approach to the problem and follow through on it. This can include direct action or a carefully thought through wait-and-see strategy.

- When you do act on your plan, monitor the implications of your actions as they begin to emerge. Be ready to revise your strategy at a moments' notice if the situation requires it and be ready to shift your strategy, analysis or statement of the problem, as more information becomes available.

Internalize Intellectual Standards: Each week, make a goal of developing one of the universal intellectual standards. These are clarity, precision, accuracy, relevance, depth, breadth, logicalness and significance. There are a few actions you can take for each standard:

- State what you are saying explicitly and precisely
- Elaborate on your meaning in other words
- Give examples from experiences you have had
- Use analogies, metaphors, pictures or diagrams to demonstrate what you mean.

Keep an Intellectual Journal: Journaling is a great way to keep track of your progress and reflect on actions you have taken. Every week, you should write a certain number of journal entries using this format:

- Describe a situation that still is or used to be emotionally significant to you.
- Describe your response to that situation.
- Analyze what exactly was going on in that situation.
- Assess the implications of the analysis and write out what you learned about yourself and what you would do differently next time.

Reshape Your Character: Choose an intellectual trait such as intellectual perseverance, autonomy, empathy, courage or humility, to strive to change each month. While you are working on that trait, focus on how you can develop it within yourself. For example, if you choose courage, you can start by determining what situations or things make you afraid or anxious and then practice slowly exposing yourself to those things.

Deal with Your Ego: Everyone has some level of an ego; some people's ego is greater than others. Keeping your ego in check is imperative to critical thinking. Put this into practice by observing your own egocentric actions or thinking by asking yourself that following questions: under what circumstances do I think with a bias in favor of myself, did I ever become irritable over small things, did I do or say anything "irrational" to get my way, did I try to impose my will upon others and did I ever fail to speak my mind when I felt strongly about something, and then later feel resentment?

After that, think of ways to replace that thinking with more rational thought and systematic self-reflection. Here, ask yourself: what would a rational person feel in this or that situation, what would a rational person do and how does that compare with what I want to do?

Redefine the Way You See Things: Every situation is given a meaning and everyone sees situations differently based on their own perspective and personal experience. How people define a situation determines how we feel about it, how we act on it and what it means for us. In that case, if you aim to see things in a more positive light, you will respond to them in a more positive and proactive way.

The first things you can do in this case is create guidelines for yourself. Create a list of five to 10 recurring negative contexts that make you feel frustrated, angry, unhappy or worried. Then identify what it is about each case that is at the root of the negative emotion that you feel. Finally, choose an alternative definition for each context and then plan for new responses and new emotions.

Get in Touch with Your Emotions: Whenever you feel a negative emotion, take the chance to pull back and ask yourself a few questions in order to redirect it into something positive. Ask yourself what the thinking is leading to this emotion and how you can change it. So, for example, if you are angry you can ask yourself those questions and determine that a co-worker is being rude. However, you can turn it around and think that they might be going through something personal and you should try not to let it get to you and instead be kind to them.

Analyze Group Influences on Your Life: Most of the time, the people you hang out with have some influence on your life whether they influence your specific actions or your outlook on life. In groups you are a part of; closely analyze the behavior that is encouraged and discouraged. Analyze factors such as what you are required to believe in these groups and what you are forbidden to do. Determine what pressure you are succumbing to and whether it is worthwhile to continue.[20]

Conclusion

Critical thinking is vital in today's world. It does not matter what profession you go into or what life situation you find yourself in, critical thinking plays an important role in each of them and the stronger your critical thinking skills are, the better equipped you will be to make the best decisions for yourself.

Some professions such as doctors and lawyers especially require critical thinking because their decisions have major implications for the lives of the people they are working with or representing. When running a business, critical thinking is also imperative to the decisions made that keep the company running long term.

Not only is critical thinking important to your success in the workforce, but it is also the key to unlocking your potential in your personal life. From making major life decisions to minor daily decisions and not questioning yourself in between, critical thinking ensures that your mind is organized and you can decipher and examine every situation you encounter adequately.

Critical thinkers add value to reasoning by creating universal questions. Applying the 5W's and H questions to nearly anything, the critical thinker can analyze and find clarity in any decision and situation. By opening the mind and moving away from passive thinking, people who regularly utilize critical thinking can have a massive impact on not only themselves but on society as a whole.

Like anything, critical thinking skills do not appear overnight. To go from the unreflective thinker to the master thinker takes time and practice. By following the steps in the critical thinking process every day and using daily strategies to strengthen your critical thinking skills, you will find that, with time, a new level of thinking is unleashed.

References

1. Baer, Andrew. "How Critical Thinking Relates to Criminal Justice." (2018). Career Trend.

2. Batmanabane, Gitanjali. Kar, SitanshuSekar. Menon, Vikas. Zayapragassarazan, Zayabalaradjane. "Understanding Critical Thinking to Create Better Doctors." (2016). Journal of Advances in Medical Education and Research.

3. "Benefits of Critical Thinking." (2019). Critical Thinking Academy.

4. Chan, Jonathan. Lau, Joe. "What Is Critical Thinking?" (2004). Critical Thinking Web.

5. Christenbury, Leila. Kelly, Patricia P. (1983). Questioning: A Path To Critical Thinking.

6. "Critical Thinking: Basic Questions & Answers." The Foundation For Critical Thinking.

7. De Sena, Joe. "Six Lessons in Critical Thinking from a Professional Critical Thinker." (2015). HuffPost.

8. "Fields of Law." Law School Admission Council.

9. Foley, Joe. "A Simple, Sure-fire Way to Create Great Content – The 5 W's & the H." (2011). WPMUDEV.

10. Groopman, Jerome. Hartzband, Pamela. "Mindful Medicine: Critical thinking leads to right diagnosis." (2008). ACP Internist.

11. "Grounding Techniques." Peirsac.

12. Half, Robert. "Accounting Skills You Need to Succeed On the Job." (2018). Robert Half.

13. Hall, Harriet. "Critical Thinking in Medicine." (2019). Science-Based Medicine.

14. "Importance of Analytical Skills in Criminal Justice." (2016). Lamar University.

15. Kaufman, James C. "Channeling Dr. House as I teach Critical Thinking." (2009). Psychology Today.

16. "Learning Critical thinking is not optional, but essential for good decision making." (2019). Critical Thinking Academy.

17. Lee, Courtney. Legal Skills For Law School & Legal Practice.

18. McKeown, Kevin. "Thinking Like A Lawyer Is A Technique - Not A Lifestyle." (2014). Above The Law.

19. Nappi, Judith S. "The Importance of Questioning in Developing Critical Thinking Skills." The Delta Kappa Gamma Bulletin: International Journal for Professional Educators.

20. Paul, R. Elder, L."Critical Thinking in Everyday Life: 9 Strategies." (2001). The Foundation For Critical Thinking.

21. Paul, R. Elder, L. "The Critical Mind is A Questioning Mind." (1996). The Foundation For Critical Thinking.

22. Portman, Janet. "Deliberations in the Jury Room." Lawyers.

23. Root, George N. "What Are the Benefits of Critical Thinking in the Workplace?" Chron.

24. Rosavich, Anne. "How to spot a job applicant with critical thinking skills." Accounting Jobs Today.

25. Ruenzel, David. "Embracing Teachers as Critical Thinkers." (2014). Education Week.

26. "Three Compelling Reasons to Learn Critical Thinking." (2019). Critical Thinking Academy.

27. Ward, Robert. "Valuing Critical Thinking in Teachers." (2018). Advancement Courses.

28. Wiley, Sandra. "5 strategies to grow critical thinking skills." (2015). Journal Of Accountancy.

29. "A Systematic Process For Critical Thinking." University of Florida.

Disclaimer

The information contained in this book and its components, is meant to serve as a comprehensive collection of strategies that the author of this book has done research about. Summaries, strategies, tips and tricks are only recommendations by the author, and reading this book will not guarantee that one's results will exactly mirror the author's results.

The author of this book has made all reasonable efforts to provide current and accurate information for the readers of this book. The author and its associates will not be held liable for any unintentional errors or omissions that may be found.

The material in the book may include information by third parties. Third party materials comprise of opinions expressed by their owners. As such, the author of this book does not assume responsibility or liability for any third party material or opinions.

without the written expressed and signed permission from the author.